BEFORE

You Get Your Puppy

BEFORE
You Get Your Puppy

Dr. Ian Dunbar

James & Kenneth
PUBLISHERS

BEFORE You Get Your Puppy
© 2001 Ian Dunbar

First published in 2001 by:

James & Kenneth Publishers
2140 Shattuck Avenue #2406
Berkeley, California 94704
1-800-784-5531

James & Kenneth - Canada
P O Box 14, Palgrave
Ontario LON 1PO
1-905-880-7502

James & Kenneth - UK
P O Box 111, Harpenden
Hertfordshire AL5 2GD
01582-715765

James & Kenneth - OZ
65 Medway Road
Bringelly NSW 2171
02-4774-9324

Printed in the United States of America

IBSN 1-888047-00-3

Dedication

The Caledon Hills

Photo Credits
Darlene Bishop: page 25
Kelly Gorman: page 44
Wayne Hightower: pages 36, 38
Carmen Noradunghian: page 79
TVS Television: page 23
Joel Walton: page 104
All other photographs were taken by the author.

Front Cover Concept by Nancy Paynter
Front Cover Illustration by Tracy Dockray
Front Cover Design by Quark & Bark Late Night Graphics Co.
Back Cover Design by Montessaurus Media

Contents

Foreword...9
Synopsis...11

Chapter One:
DEVELOPMENTAL DEADLINES ..15
1. Your Doggy Education 20
2. Evaluating Puppy's Progress 21
3. Errorless Housetraining 22
4. Socialization with People 23
5. Bite Inhibition.............................24
6. The Great Outdoors 25

Chapter Two:
YOUR DOGGY EDUCATION.........27
Which Type of Dog 30
Mixed Breed or Pure Breed? 32
Which Breed? 33
Movie DogStars................................37
When to Get a Puppy........................39
Where to Get a Puppy 41
How to Select a Good Breeder..........41
Puppy vs. Adult 43
Shopping List...................................46

Chapter Three:
EVALUATING PUPPY'S PROGRESS..47
How to Select a Good Puppy 48
Handling and Gentling......................49
Sound Sensitivity.............................50
Household Etiquette 51
Basic Manners 52
Personal Preference 52
Singleton Pups 54

Chapter Four:
ERRORLESS HOUSETRAINING 57
When You Are Not at Home..............58
Long-term Confinement 60
When You Are at Home.....................60
Short-term Confinement 61
Train Your Puppy to Train Itself........63
Errorless Housetraining 63
Housetraining 1-2-3 64
So What's the Problem?.....................65
Doggy Toilet 74
Errorless Chewtoy-Training 75
What Is a Chewtoy?..........................77
Dinner from Chewtoys 78
Chewtoy Stuffing..............................80
Kong Stuffing 101 81
Settle Down and Shush.....................82
What to Do at Nighttime 85
Sit, etc. 86
Misbehavior 89

Chapter Five:
PUPPY PRIORITIES 91

Chapter Six:
BOOKS and VIDEOS 100

To all truly exceptional dog breeders, who care as much (if not more) about their dogs' physical and mental health as they do about their dogs' coat color and conformation.

To all knowledgeable veterinarians, who understand the crucially important role of early socialization and training for the prevention of predictable behavior and temperament problems.

To all caring and responsible puppy owners, who did their very best to choose, raise, and train their puppies to be good-natured and well-mannered companions.

And to all overworked pet dog trainers, shelter staff and volunteers, and animal rescue organizations, who try their best to solve the many problems created by other dog breeders, veterinarians, and dog owners who failed to grasp the big picture.

Foreword

Sadly, the majority of puppies fail to live long enough to enjoy their second birthday. Their terminal illness is being unwanted —failing to live up to the promise and expectation of the Lassie–Benji–Eddie dream. Instead they develop a number of utterly predictable behavior, training, and temperament problems and are surrendered to animal shelters to play the lotto of life. Many people like to shift the blame and cite irresponsible ownership. I would cite lack of know-how. Most prospective puppy owners are simply unaware of the types of problems that lay ahead, nor do they know how to prevent or resolve them. Ironically, the demise of many dogs stems from novice owners following misleading, erroneous and in some cases, downright bad advice from out-of-date training books.

Dog owners' lack of know-how has to be the responsibility of all doggy professionals, including dog breeders, trainers, veterinarians, animal control officers, and shelter personnel. It is the fault of dog professionals like myself, who have failed to adequately advertise that there is a much easier, quicker, gentler, and altogether more effective and efficient way to raise and train puppies.

This booklet lists common, predictable puppy problems, provides a timetable for their development, and suggests a variety of dog-friendly preventative measures and solutions. It emphasizes the overwhelming importance of early socialization, confinement, prevention, reward training, and lure/reward training techniques.

Feeling that education can range from boring to hilarious, I have always striven to make my writing enjoyable as well as informative. However, there is always a delicate balance between education and entertainment. When writing the previous edition of this booklet (previously published as *The New PuppyDog*), I did not deliver the goods. The humor was there, but the facts were camouflaged. The text lacked the necessary emphasis and urgency and did not say what it should have said. This was a great shame, considering the extreme importance and overwhelming urgency of the intended topic.

My sincere thanks go to Jane Stevenson and Dr. Bruce Boehringer for their extremely constructive and critical reviews of the original manuscript, which more than sufficiently pointed out its shortcomings. Thank you both! This booklet is a complete rewrite. I am indebted to Jane for her unwavering encouragement. Additionally, huge thanks go to Jane's Dad for his invaluable comments on this edition.

I very much hope that you find this new booklet to be as enjoyable as the last and that it adequately emphasizes the two most important and pressing points:

1. When choosing a puppy, you need to know how to determine whether its behavioral development and education are up to par. Assessing a pup's developmental and educational status depends on *your* education about puppy education.

2. Your pup's first week in your home is the most crucial developmental period of its life. This short, make-or-break period pretty much determines whether your puppy will develop into a well-mannered and good-natured companion that will bring joy to your life for many years to come, or whether your puppy will develop numerous, predictable behavior problems and grow up to be fearful and unfriendly. You stand at the crossroads. The course of your prospective puppy's development is in your hands.

Synopsis

If you have your heart set on raising and training a puppy, do make sure you train yourself beforehand. Remember, it takes only a few days to ruin an otherwise perfect puppy. Without a doubt, the most important developmental deadline comes before you even think of getting your puppy, i.e., your education about puppy education!

Many first-time puppy owners are surprised when they discover their new companion bites, barks, chews, digs, and marks the house with urine and feces. Yet these are all perfectly normal, natural, and necessary doggy behaviors.

Your canine newcomer is just itching to learn human house manners. It wants to please, but it has to know how to please. It's no good keeping house rules a secret. Somebody has to tell the dog. And that somebody is you.

Before inviting a puppy to come and share your life, surely it is only wise and fair to find out beforehand what you might expect from a normal developing puppy, which behaviors and traits you might consider unacceptable, and how to modify the pup's inappropriate behavior and temperament accordingly. Specifically, owners need to know how to teach the youngster where to eliminate, what to chew, when to bark, where to dig, to sit when greeting people, to walk calmly on-leash, to settle down and shush when requested, to inhibit its otherwise quite normal biting behavior, and to thoroughly enjoy the company of other dogs and people—especially strangers and children.

Whether selecting your prospective pup from a professional breeder or from a family breeding a litter for the very first time, the criteria are the same. Look for puppies which have been raised indoors around human companionship and influence: i.e., around people who have devoted lots of time to the puppies' education.

Your puppy needs to be prepared for the clamor of everyday domestic living - the noise of the vacuum cleaner, pots and pans dropping in the kitchen, sports programs screaming on the television, children crying, and adults arguing. Exposure to such stimuli while its eyes and ears are still developing allows the puppy (with blurred vision and muffled hearing) to gradually become accustomed to sights and sounds that might otherwise frighten it when older.

Avoid pups which have been raised in an outdoor run or kennel. Remember, you want a puppy to share your home, so look for a puppy that has been raised in a home. Basement- and kennel-raised puppies are certainly not pet-quality dogs. They are "livestock" on par with veal calves and battery hens. They are neither housetrained nor socialized, and they do not make good companions. Look for litters which have been born and raised in a kitchen or living room.

Choosing a breed is a very personal choice—your choice. But you will save yourself a lot of unnecessary problems and heartbreak if your choice is an informed and educated one. Choose the breed you like, investigate breed-specific qualities and problems, and then research the best way to raise and train it. Make sure you test drive several adult dogs of your selected breed or type before you make your final choice. Test driving adult dogs will quickly teach you everything you need to know about a specific breed. Test driving adult dogs will also pinpoint the gaps in your education concerning dog behavior and training.

Regardless of your choice, please do not kid yourself that all you have to do is select the "perfect" breed and the "perfect" individual and the puppy will automatically grow up into the "perfect" adult dog. Any puppy can become a marvelous companion if appropriately socialized and trained. And, no matter what its breed or breeding, any puppy can become a doggy delinquent if not properly socialized and trained. Please make an intelligent, researched choice when selecting your puppy, but remember: appropriate socialization and training is the single biggest factor which determines how closely the dog will approach your view of perfection in adulthood.

Irrespective of your eventual choice—and certainly once you have made it—success or failure is entirely in your hands. Your puppy's behavior and temperament now depend one hundred percent on good husbandry and training.

Your puppy's living quarters need to be designed so that housetraining and chewtoy training are errorless. Each mistake is a potential disaster, since it heralds many more to come.

Long-term confinement prevents your puppy from learning to make mistakes around the house, and allows your puppy to teach itself to use an appropriate toilet, to settle down quietly and calmly, and to want to chew appropriate chewtoys. Confinement with chewtoys stuffed with kibble and treats teaches your puppy to enjoy its own company and prepares it for those times when it might be left at home alone.

Short-term close confinement also prevents your puppy from learning to make mistakes around the house, and allows your puppy to teach itself to settle down quietly and calmly, and to want to chew appropriate chewtoys. Additionally, short-term confinement enables you to accurately predict *when* your puppy needs to relieve itself, so that you may take your puppy to an appropriate toilet area and reward it for using it. The knack of successful housetraining focuses on being able to predict when your puppy "wants to go."

Your puppy's playroom (long-term confinement area) requires a comfortable bed, a fresh supply of water, a chewtoy, and a toilet.

Before You Get Your Puppy

If you are thinking of welcoming a new puppy into your home, this booklet could well be the most important one that you ever read. It comprises what you must know before choosing a puppy and what you must teach your puppy during its very first week at home.

From the moment you choose your puppy, there is some considerable urgency regarding socialization and training. There is no time to waste. Basically, an adult dog's temperament and behavior habits (both good and bad) are shaped during puppyhood—very early puppyhood. In fact, some puppies are well on their way to ruin by the time they are just eight weeks old. It is especially easy to make horrendous mistakes when selecting a pup and during its first few days at home. Such mistakes usually have an indelible effect, influencing your pup's behavior and temperament for the rest of its life. This is not to say that unsocialized and untrained eight-week-old pups cannot be rehabilitated. They can, if you work quickly. But whereas it is so easy to prevent behavior and temperament problems from the beginning, rehabilitation can be both difficult and time-consuming, and it is unlikely that your pup will ever become the adult dog it could have been.

Learn how to make intelligent choices when selecting your pup. Learn how to implement a course of errorless housetraining and errorless chewtoy-training the moment your puppy arrives at its new home. Any housesoiling or chewing mistake you allow your puppy to make is absolute silliness and absolute seriousness: silliness because you are creating lots of future headaches for yourself, and seriousness because millions

Nancy's house after a Shepherd party! Chewtoys stuffed with food would provide the dogs with appropriate amusement and occupational therapy to pass the time when left at home alone.

of dogs are euthanized each year simply because their owners did not know how to housetrain or chewtoy-train them.

If your pup is *ever* left unsupervised indoors it will most certainly chew household articles and soil your house. Although these teeny accidents do little damage in themselves, they set the precedent for your puppy's choice of toys and toilets for many months to come.

Any puppy housesoiling or house-destruction mistake is a potential disaster, since it predicts numerous future mistakes from a dog with larger bladder and bowels and much more destructive jaws. Many owners begin to notice their puppy's destructiveness by the time it is four to five months old, when the pup is characteristically relegated outdoors. Destruction is the product of a puppy's boredom, lack of supervision, and a

Allowing a single housesoiling mistake is a disaster since it sets the precedent for your puppy's toilet area and signals many more mistakes to come.

search for entertainment. Natural inquisitiveness prompts the lonely pup to dig, escape, and bark in its quest for some form of occupational therapy to pass the time of day in solitary confinement. Once the neighbors complain about the dog's incessant barking and periodic escapes, the dog is often further confined to a garage or basement. Usually though, this is only

Digging, barking, and escaping are usually secondary problems of unhousetrained adolescent dogs which have been relegated to a life of solitary confinement and boredom in the yard. Housetrain your dog, and then you may leave it indoors. Magically, the digging and escaping problems will disappear.

17

One of the best ways to reduce excessive barking is to teach your puppy to speak on cue. Training your pup to bark on request facilitates teaching it to shush on request, since you may now shush-train the pup at your convenience. Instead of trying to quieten your puppy when it is excitedly barking, you may request your pup to bark and so teach shush at times when the pup is calm and focussed.

a temporary measure until the dog is surrendered to a local animal shelter to play the lotto of life. Fewer than 25 percent of surrendered dogs are adopted, of which about half are returned as soon as the new owners discover their adopted adolescent's annoying problems.

The above summarizes the fate of many dogs. This is especially sad because all these simple problems could be prevented so easily. Housetraining and chewtoy-training are hardly rocket science. But you do need to know what to do. And you need to know what to do *before* you bring your puppy home.

Developmental Deadlines

As soon as your puppy comes home, the clock is running. Within just three months, your puppy will need to meet six crucial developmental deadlines. If your puppy fails to meet any of these deadlines, it will be unlikely to achieve its full potential. In terms of your dog's behavior and temperament, you will probably be playing catch-up for the rest of your dog's life. You simply cannot afford to neglect the socialization and bite inhibition deadlines.

1. **Your Doggy Education** (before searching)
2. **Evaluating Puppy's Progress** (before selection)
3. **Errorless Housetraining** (before homecoming)
4. **Socialization with People** (by 12 weeks of age)
5. **Bite Inhibition** (by 18 weeks of age)
6. **The Great Outdoors** (by five months of age)

If you already have a puppy and feel that you are behind, do not throw in the towel. You must acknowledge, however, that you are well behind and that your puppy's socialization and education are now a dire emergency. Immediately do your best to catch up. Contact a pet dog trainer immediately. To locate a trainer in your area, call 1-800-PET-DOGS for the Association of Pet Dog Trainers. Invite family, friends, and neighbors to help you with your puppy's remedial socialization and training. Maybe take a week or two off of work to devote to your puppy. The younger your puppy, the easier and quicker it is to catch up on its developmental timetable and minimize losses. However, every day you delay makes it harder.

1. *Your Doggy Education*

*Planning for a new puppy begins with
the owner's education about puppy education.*

Before you look for your perfect puppy, you need to know what
sort of dog to look for, where to get it, and when to get it. An
educated choice is generally far better than an impulsive puppy
purchase. Additionally, you need to thoroughly familiarize
yourself with the developmental deadlines; they become urgent
and crucial the day you select your puppy. Take your time to
review this booklet and then make a thoughtful choice because
your dog's future depends on it.

2. Evaluating Puppy's Progress

Before you select your puppy (usually at eight weeks of age), you need to know how to select a good breeder and how to select a good puppy. Specifically, you need to know how to assess your puppy's behavioral development. By eight weeks of age: your puppy must have become thoroughly accustomed to a home physical environment, especially to all sorts of potentially scary noises; your puppy should already be well-socialized and have been handled by many people, especially men and children; your puppy's errorless housetraining and chewtoy training should be under way; and your puppy should already have a rudimentary understanding of basic manners. At the very least, your puppy should come, sit, lie down, and rollover when requested. In other words, in preparation for household living, the litter of puppies must have been raised indoors and around people and not in some secluded backyard or kennel.

This candidate for Rocky Mountain Search and Rescue was carefully selected at eight weeks of age from a carefully selected litter.

3. *Errorless Housetraining*

You need to ensure that an errorless housetraining and chewtoy-training program is instituted the very first day your puppy comes home. This is so important during the first week, when puppies characteristically learn good or bad habits which set the precedent for weeks, months, and sometimes years to come.

Be absolutely certain that you fully understand the principles of long-term and short-term confinement before you bring your new puppy home. With a long-term and short-term confinement schedule, housetraining and chewtoy-training are easy,

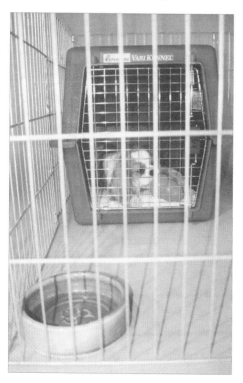

efficient, and errorless. During its first few weeks at home, regular confinement (with chewtoys stuffed with kibble) teaches the puppy to teach itself to chew chewtoys, to settle down calmly and quietly, and not to become a recreational barker. Moreover, short-term confinement allows you to predict when your puppy needs to relieve itself, so that you may take it to the right spot and reward it for eliminating.

4. Socialization with People

Puppies must be socialized to people, especially men and children, before they are three months old.

The Critical Period of Socialization ends by three months of age. This is the crucial developmental stage during which puppies learn to accept and enjoy the company of other dogs and people. Thus your puppy needs to be socialized to people by the time it is twelve weeks old. However, since its series of puppy immunization injections is incomplete at this point, a young pup needs to meet people in the safety of its own home. As a rule of thumb, your puppy needs to meet at least a hundred different people during its first month at home. Not only is this easier to do than it might sound, it's also lots of fun.

5. Bite Inhibition

Bite inhibition is the single most important lesson a dog must learn. Adult dogs have teeth and jaws which can hurt and harm. All animals must learn to inhibit use of their weapons against their own kind, but domestic animals must learn to be gentle with all animals, especially people. Domestic dogs must learn to inhibit their biting towards all animals, especially towards other dogs and people. The narrow time window for developing a soft mouth begins to close at four-and-a-half months of age, about the time when the adult canine teeth first show. Providing your puppy with an ideal forum to learn bite inhibition is the most pressing reason to enroll it in puppy classes before it is eighteen weeks old.

Bite inhibition is all-important. Puppies must learn to inhibit the force of their biting before they are taught to stop biting and mouthing altogether.

6. The Great Outdoors

Maintaining socialization requires ongoing socialization throughout puppyhood, adolescence, and adulthood. Your dog will continue to gain confidence with continued exposure to unfamiliar people, to unfamiliar dogs, and to unfamiliar situations.

To ensure that your well-rounded and well-schooled puppy remains a mannerly, well-socialized, and friendly dog throughout adulthood, your dog needs to meet unfamiliar people and unfamiliar dogs on a regular basis, i.e., your dog needs to be walked at least once a day. Your puppy may be taken for rides in the car and to visit friends' houses as early as you like. Start walking your puppy as soon as your veterinarian says it is safe to do so.

BEFORE You Get Your Puppy addresses the first three developmental deadlines, covering the search and selection for a suitable puppy and its first week at home. The first three developmental deadlines are extremely urgent and crucial, and leave no room for mistakes. A second booklet—*AFTER You Get Your Puppy*—addresses the final three developmental deadlines, covering the first three months the puppy is in your home. The clock is still running, but you do have three months to get things done.

A Rolls Royce doggy personality
requires a Rolls Royce owner education.

First Developmental Deadline
(Before You Search for Your Puppy)

Your Doggy Education

Without a doubt the most important developmental deadline comes before you even think of getting your puppy, namely, your education about puppy education! Just as you would learn how to drive before setting off in a car, it would be similarly prudent to learn how to raise and train a puppy before you get one.

Some owners want heaven and earth from their pups; others only demand magic and miracles. Owners want the puppy to be perfectly well-behaved and to amuse itself when left at home alone for hours on end. And they assume the pup will magically grow up to act this way without guidance.

It is simply not fair to keep house rules a secret from your puppy, only to moan and groan when it predictably finds doggy ways to entertain itself and break rules it didn't even know existed. If you have house rules, somebody needs to teach them to the puppy. And that somebody is you.

Luckily, dogs have their natural activity peaks at dawn and dusk, so many are quite happy to settle down and snooze the day away. However, some dogs are not. In fact, some dogs are more active, and when left at home alone become exceedingly stressed and may destroy the house and garden in the space of a day.

Puppy owners are often surprised when their new puppy bites, barks, chews, digs, and decorates the floors with urine and feces. Yet this is what dogs do. How did you expect your dog to speak? To moo? To meow? And what did you expect your dog to do to pass the time of day? Housework? To mop and clean floors and dust the furniture? Or to amuse itself reading books, watching television, or doing macrame?

Many owners appear to be at a further loss when confronted by utterly predictable problems, such as jumping up, pulling on-leash, and expressing the boundless energy and exuberance accompanying doggy adolescence. Additionally, owners are incredulous if their adolescent or adult dog bites or fights. When dogs are undersocialized, harassed, abused, frightened, or otherwise upset, what do we expect them to do? Call a lawyer? Of course they bite! Biting is as normal an ingredient of canine behavior as wagging the tail or burying a bone.

Before inviting a puppy to come and share your life, surely it is only wise and fair to find out beforehand what you might expect from a normal developing puppy, which behaviors and

Dogs are dogs. Not surprisingly, puppies behave like dogs: they chew, dig, bark, communicate largely via body language and p-mail, and spend much of their free time sniffing rear ends.

traits you might consider unacceptable, and how to modify the pup's inappropriate behavior and temperament accordingly. Specifically, owners need to know how to teach the youngster when to bark, what to chew, where to dig, where to perform its toilet duties, to sit when greeting people, to walk calmly on-leash, to settle down and shush when requested, to inhibit its otherwise quite normal biting behavior, and to thoroughly enjoy the company of other dogs and of people, especially men, strangers, and children.

It is vital that you know *what* and *how* to teach your puppy, *before* you get it. So read books, watch videos, observe puppy training classes, and above all, test drive as many adult dogs as possible. Talk to owners at puppy class and discover what types of problems they are experiencing. New puppy owners are ruthlessly honest when describing their puppy's problems.

Which Type of Dog?

There are many things to consider when choosing a puppy, including which breed or type, and the optimum age of acquisition. Obviously, you want to choose a dog that is best

suited to you and your lifestyle. Rather than offering specific recommendations, I will list some of the more important guidelines.

First, please do not kid yourself that all you have to do is select the "perfect" breed and the "perfect"

individual puppy and it will automatically grow up into the "perfect" adult dog. Any puppy can become a marvelous companion if appropriately socialized and trained. And, no matter what its breed or breeding, any puppy can become a doggy delinquent if not properly socialized and trained. Please make an intelligent, researched choice when selecting your puppy, but remember: appropriate socialization and training is the single biggest factor which determines how closely the dog will approach your view of perfection in adulthood.

Second, seek advice from the best sources. Common mistakes are to take breed advice from veterinarians, health advice from breeders, and all-important behavior and training advice from veterinarians, breeders, and pet-store personnel. The best plan is to seek training and behavior advice from trainers and behavior counselors, health advice from veterinarians, breed advice from breeders, and product advice from pet-store personnel. And if you really want to know what's going on, check out a local puppy class and chat with the owners; they'll give you the cold, hard facts regarding what it's really like to live with a puppy.

Third, evaluate all advice carefully. Apply the common sense principle: does it make sense to you? Is the advice relevant to your family and your lifestyle? Whereas most advice is sound, some can be irrelevant, hypocritical, preachy or questionable. And occasionally, "advice" can be just downright bad.

Example 1: One breeder told a couple they could not buy a puppy unless they had a fenced yard and one of them was home all day. Yet the breeder herself had no fenced yard and her twenty or so dogs lived in crates in a kennel a good forty yards away from her house and any hope of human companionship. Duh!??

Example 2: Many people are advised not to get a large dog if they live in an apartment. On the contrary! As long as they receive regular walks, large dogs make wonderful apartment companions. Compared with smaller dogs, large dogs seem to settle down better and tend to bark less. Many little dogs exasperate owners and neighbors by being active and noisy, and running amuck. However, smaller dogs make wonderful apartment companions so long as they are trained to settle down and shush.

Example 3: Many veterinarians advise that Golden Retrievers and Labrador Retrievers are the best dogs with children. All breeds of dog may make good companions for children, provided that they have been trained how to act around children, and provided that the children have been taught how to act around dogs! Otherwise, dogs—including Goldens and Labs—are likely to be frightened and irritated by children, or excited and incited by their antics.

Remember, you are selecting a puppy to live with you for a good long time. Choosing a puppy to share your life is a very personal choice - your choice. You will save yourself a lot of unnecessary problems and heartbreak if your choice is an informed and educated one.

In reality though, people seldom pay heed to well-meant advice and usually end up choosing with heart instead of head. Indeed many people end up choosing a dog along the same lines as they might choose a lifelong human companion: on the basis of coat color, conformation, and cuteness. But regardless of the many reasons for selecting a particular puppy, whether based on pedigree, conformation, cuteness, or general health, the success of the endeavor ultimately depends almost entirely on the pup's education regarding appropriate behavior and training.

Mixed Breed or Pure Breed?

Again, this decision is a personal choice that only you can make. The most obvious difference is that pure breeds are more predictable in terms of looks and behavior, whereas each mixed breed is utterly unique —one of a kind.

Regardless of your personal preference for attractiveness, attentiveness, and activity, you would do well to consider general health and life expectancy. By and large, due to lack of inbreeding, mixed breeds are healthier genetic stock; they tend to live longer and have fewer health problems. On the other hand, at a pure-breed kennel, it is possible to check out the friendliness, basic manners, general health, and life expectancy of several generations of your prospective puppy's forebears.

Which Breed?

I am strongly opposed to suggesting breeds for people. Recommending specific breeds may sound like helpful and harmless advice, but it is insidiously dangerous and not in the best interests of dogs or of dog-owning families. Advice either for or against specific breeds often leads owners to believe that training is either unnecessary or impossible. Thus many poor dogs grow up without an education.

Breed recommendations often lead unsuspecting owners to believe that once they have selected the right breed, there is nothing more to do. Thinking they have the best possible breed, many owners suffer the misconception that training is unnecessary and so don't bother. This of course is when things start to go downhill.

Even more disturbing, when certain breeds are recommended, other breeds are automatically being advised against. "Experts" often suggest that certain breeds are too big, too small, too active, too lethargic, too fast, too slow, too smart, or too dumb, and therefore too difficult to train. Well, we know that regardless of helpful "advice," people are probably going to pick the breed they wanted in the first place. But now they may feel disinclined to train the puppy, feeling that the process is going to be difficult and time consuming. Furthermore, owners may rationalize their negligence by citing any of the pack of convenient excuses listed above.

Breed is a very personal choice. Choose the breed you like, investigate breed-specific qualities and problems, and then research the best way to raise and train your pup. If you select what others consider to be an easy breed to raise and train, train it so that it becomes the very best individual of that breed —an ambassador for the breed of your choice. And if you select a breed that some people consider difficult to raise and train, train it, train it, and train it, so that it becomes the very best example of the breed—an ambassador for the breed of your choice.

Regardless of your eventual choice of breed, and certainly once you have made it, success or failure is now entirely in your hands. Your puppy's behavior and temperament now depend one hundred percent on good husbandry and training.

When evaluating different breeds, the good points are obvious. What you need to find out are the breed's bad points. You need to investigate potential breed-specific (or line-specific) problems and to know how to deal with them. If you want to find out more about a specific breed's good points and bad points, find at least six adult dogs of the breed you have selected. Talk to their owners at length, but most importantly,

meet the dogs! Examine and handle them; play with them and work them. See if the dogs welcome being petted by a stranger (i.e., you). Will they sit? Do they walk nicely on leash? Are they quiet or noisy? Are they calm and collected, or are they hyperactive and rambunctious? Can you examine their ears, eyes, and rear end? Can you open their muzzle? Can you get them to roll over? Are the owners' houses and gardens still in good condition? And most importantly, do the dogs like people and other dogs?

It is smart to know what to expect because when your eight-week-old puppy comes home, you will find it grows up with frightening speed. In fact, in just four months time your pup will develop into a six-month-old adolescent that has gained almost adult size, strength, and speed, while at the same time retaining many puppy constraints on learning. There is just so much to teach your puppy before it collides with impending adolescence.

In terms of personality, behavior, and temperament, please be aware that dogs of the same breed may show considerable

Basic handling exercises are the most important aspect of "test driving" different dogs. Make sure each dog enjoys being gently restrained (snuggled, cuddled, and hugged) as you examine its ears, muzzle, and paws.

variation. If you have siblings or more than one child you probably appreciate the incredible range of temperaments and personalities of children from the same parents. Dogs are similar. Indeed, there may be as much variation of behavior traits among individuals from the same litter as there is among dogs of different breeds.

Environmental influences (socialization and training) exert a far greater impact on desired domestic behavior and temperament than genetic heredity. For example, the temperamental differences between a good (educated) Malamute and a bad (uneducated) Malamute or between a good Golden and a bad Golden are much greater than temperamental differences between a Golden and a Malamute with an equivalent experiential and educational history. A dog's education (socialization and training) is always the biggest factor determining its future behavior and temperament.

Please make sure you fully understand the above paragraph. I am not saying training necessarily has a greater effect on dog behavior than genetic heredity. Rather, I am stating quite categorically that desired domestic dog

The author with DogStar Moose and trainer Mathilde DeCagny at the Association of Pet Dog Trainers' Conference in San Diego.

behavior is almost entirely dependent on socialization and training. For example, dogs bark, bite, urine mark, and wag their tails largely for genetic reasons—because they are dogs. However, the frequency of their barks, the severity of their bites, the location of their urine marks and the enthusiasm of their tail wags depends pretty much on the nature of their socialization and training. Your dog's domestic success is in your hands.

Movie DogStars

When selecting a breed, don't be duped by celebrity dogs appearing in films or on television. These dogs are highly trained canine actors. In fact, Lassie has been played by at least eight different canine actors. The dogs are acting, and often the requirements of their role masks their true breed and individual characteristics. This is no different from Anthony Hopkins playing Hannibal Lecter in *The Silence of the Lambs* and C. S. Lewis in *Shadowlands*—two very different roles, and both of them completely different from what we may suppose is the real Anthony Hopkins. It's acting, and in a sense you need to teach your puppy how to act—that is, how to act appropriately in a variety of domestic settings, such as the living room and the park.

Eddie (Moose) appears to be calm and controlled on the set of *Frasier*, because Moose The Active was trained to be calm and controlled to play the role of Eddie. Moreover, Eddie's endearing television demeanor and his acquired social savvy, charming manners, and acting skills have successfully overcome his original delinquent disposition.

Here follows an extract from "Doggy Dialogues"—an interview between yours truly, Moose, and his trainer, Mathilde DeCagny.

(Excerpts from "Doggy Dialogues" are reprinted from *The Bark* with permission of the publishers.)

ID: What is Moose really like?

MD: Moose has his own personality! I got him when he was about two years old and he was a terror—a tyrant —selfish and mischievous with lots of negativity. He'd constantly try to escape, he'd chase squirrels, he'd get into trash and into dog fights. His recall was nonexistent. I could never get him to come back to me. And I wasn't the first one who had tried. He would pee everywhere and he was just very, very…

ID: He sounds like a normal human movie star.

MD: Absolutely! But he's changed so much. He's a different dog. He's interested in training and he loves the idea of being busy. He has always been impatient —no patience whatsoever. It was always Moose, Moose, Moose—right now, right now. So through the years I've taught him to be more patient and to be a little nicer with me. Originally he was extremely independent and didn't care about being petted. He had owners before me who just couldn't cope with him because there was no giving on his end. Now he's very affectionate.

When to Get a Puppy

Aside from the obvious answer—not before you are ready—the time to get a dog is when you have completed your doggy education.

An important consideration is the age of the pup. Most puppies change homes at some time in their life, usually from the original home (where they were born) to new homes shared with their new human companions. The optimal time for a puppy to change homes depends on many variables, including its emotional needs, its all-important socialization schedule, and the level of doggy expertise in each household.

Leaving home can be traumatic, and limiting the pup's emotional trauma is a prime consideration. If the puppy leaves home too early, it will miss out on early pup-pup and pup-mother interactions. And since the first weeks in a new home are often spent in a doggy social vacuum, the developing puppy may grow up undersocialized towards its own kind. On the other hand, the longer the puppy stays in its original home the more attached it becomes to its doggy family and the harder the eventual transition. A delayed transition also postpones all-important socialization with the new family.

Eight weeks of age has long been accepted as the optimal time for a new pup to be acquired. By eight weeks, sufficient dog-dog socialization has taken place with mother and litter mates to tide the puppy over until it is old enough to safely meet and play with other dogs in puppy class and dog parks and yet still be sufficiently young to form a strong bond with the members of its new family.

The relative level of doggy expertise in either home is a vital consideration in determining whether the puppy is better off staying longer in its original home or leaving earlier to live with its new owners. It is often assumed that breeders are experts and owners are rank novices, so that it makes sense to leave the pup with the breeder for as long as possible. A conscientious breeder is usually better qualified to socialize, housetrain, and chewtoy-train the puppy. When this is true, it makes sense to get the puppy when it is older. (In fact, I often ask novice owners whether they have considered a socially mature and well-trained adult dog as an alternative to a young pup.)

This of course presupposes the breeder's superior expertise. Unfortunately, just as there are excellent, average, novice, and irresponsible owners, there are also excellent, average, novice, and irresponsible breeders. With the combination of an experienced owner and a less-than-average breeder, the puppy would be better off moving to its new home as early as possible, certainly by six to eight weeks at the latest. If you feel you are a qualified puppy raiser but the breeder will not let you take your pup home before eight weeks of age, look elsewhere. Remember, you are searching for a puppy to live with you, not with the breeder. In fact, you might be better off looking elsewhere anyway, since a less-than-average breeder probably produces less-than-average puppies.

Adopting an adult dog from an animal shelter or rescue organization can be a marvelous alternative to raising a puppy. Some shelter and rescue dogs are well trained and simply in need of a home. Others have a few behavior problems and require their puppy education in adulthood. Some dogs are purebred; most are mixed breeds. The key to finding a good shelter or rescue dog is selection, selection, selection!!! Take plenty of time to test drive each prospective candidate. Each dog is unique.

Where to Get a Puppy

Whether selecting your prospective pup from a professional breeder or from a family that is breeding a litter for the very first time, the criteria are the same. First, look for puppies which have been raised indoors around human companionship and influence. Avoid pups which have been raised in an outdoor run or kennel. Remember, you want a puppy to share your home, and so look for a puppy that has been raised in a home. Second, assess your prospective puppy's current socialization and education status. Regardless of breed, breeding, pedigree, and lineage, if your prospective puppy's socialization and training programs are not well underway by eight weeks of age, it is already developmentally retarded.

How to Select a Good Breeder

A good breeder will be extremely choosy in accepting prospective puppy buyers. A prospective owner should be equally choosy when selecting a breeder. A prospective owner can begin to evaluate a breeder's expertise by noting whether she ranks the puppies' mental well-being and physical health above their good looks. You need to determine: whether the breeder's adult dogs are all people-friendly and well-trained; whether your prospective puppy's parents, grandparents, great-grandparents, and other relations all live to a ripe old age; and whether your prospective pup is already well-socialized and well-trained.

Friendly dogs are self-apparent when you meet them, and so meet as many of your prospective puppy's relatives as possible. Friendly dogs are living proof of good socialization by a good breeder.

Beware the breeder who is only willing to show you puppies. First, a good breeder will take the time to see how you get along with adult dogs before letting you anywhere near the pups. A good breeder wouldn't let you leave with a puppy if you didn't know how to handle an adult dog, which your puppy will be in just a few months. Second, you want to evaluate as many adult dogs as possible from your prospective puppy's family and line before you let your heart be seduced by a litter of supercute puppies. If all the adult dogs are people-friendly and well-behaved, it is a good bet that you have discovered an exceptional breeder.

The nitty-gritty of evaluating different breeders centers on assessing the behavioral and temperamental aspects of their puppies and estimating their life expectancy. (See the Second Developmental Deadline.) Similarly, the search for a good puppy depends on finding a good breeder. The puppies' physique, behavior, and temperament all reflect the breeder's expertise. Thus, searching for a good breeder and the selection of an individual quality puppy pretty much go hand in hand.

The single best indicator of general health, good behavior, and temperament is the overall life expectancy of a kennel line. Check to see that your prospective puppy's parents, grandparents, great grandparents, and other relations are still alive and healthy or that they died at a ripe old age. Conscientious breeders will have telephone numbers readily available for previous puppy buyers and for the breeders of the other dogs in your prospective puppy's pedigree. If the breeder is not eager to share information regarding life expectancy and the incidence of breed-specific diseases, look elsewhere. You will eventually find a breeder who will accommodate your concerns. Before you open your heart to a young pup, you certainly want to maximize the likelihood that the two of you will be spending a long and healthy life together. Additionally, long-lived dogs advertise good temperament and training, since dogs with behavior and temperament problems generally have short life expectancies.

Puppy vs. Adult

Before rushing ahead and getting a puppy, it's a good idea to at least consider the pros and cons of adopting an adult dog. Certainly, there are several advantages to getting a pup, the foremost being that the new owners may mold the puppy's behavior and temperament to suit their own particular lifestyle. This, of course, presumes that the new owners know how to train and have the time to do it. Sometimes they don't. And so in a lot of ways an adolescent or adult dog with a Kennel Club

Little brown dog Oliver (adopted from the Chicago Heights Humane Society at nine months of age) has now graduated to NPD Status (Near Perfect Dog).

obedience title and a Canine Good Citizenship Test may make a more suitable companion—especially for a two-income family whose members barely have the time to get together as a family themselves.

"Ratweiler" Tater Tot (adopted at two years of age) was awarded 1st Place in the KPIX Late Show Stupid Pet Tricks competition and has won the K9 Games® Waltzes with Dogs competition twice.

Grizzly old Ashby (saved from the syringe at ten years of age) lived out his sunset years in some considerable comfort at Villa Phoenix.

Big red Claude (recently adopted at one year of age from the San Francisco SPCA) is still a bit of a project. But he sits beautifully for lettuce!

Additionally, a two-year-old (or older) adult dog's habits, manners, and temperament are already well-established, for better or for worse. Traits and habits may change over time, but compared with the behavioral changeability of young puppies, an older dog's good habits are as resistant to change as their bad habits. Consequently, it is possible to test drive a number of adult shelter dogs and select one free of problems and with an established personality to your liking. Please at least consider this alternative.

If you still have your heart set on raising and training a puppy, do make sure you educate yourself beforehand. Only search for a puppy *after* you have learned how to raise and train one. Remember, it takes only a few days to ruin an otherwise perfect puppy.

Whether you decide to get a puppy or adopt an adult dog, please make an appointment with your veterinarian to get your puppy/dog neutered. There are simply too many unwanted dogs. Millions are euthanized each year. Please do not add to the numbers.

45

Shopping List

Once you have completed your doggy education it is time to shop for your prospective puppy. Many training books, pet stores, and dog catalogs display an awesome and confusing array of doggy products and training equipment. Consequently, I have listed a number of essentials with personal preferences in parentheses.

1. Dog crate (Vari Kennel), and maybe an exercise pen, or baby gates as barriers
2. At least six chewtoys to stuff with kibble and treats (Kong products and bones)
3. Doggy toilet (Construct your own: see p. 74)
4. Water bowl
5. Dog food (Kibble) Note: During its first few weeks at home, make sure your puppy receives all food stuffed in chewtoys, or handfed as rewards for socialization and training. Buy your puppy a food bowl once it is socialized, well-trained, and has impeccable household manners
6. Freeze dried liver for men, strangers, and children to win your puppy's confidence and as rewards for housetraining (Benny Bully's Liver Treats)
7. Martingale collar, leash, and maybe a Gentle Leader (Premier Pet Products)

Most of the above items, plus informative books and videos (pp. 100-103) are available from your local pet store, or mail order and on-line from Best Dog Stuff at:
1-800-297-0225 or www.bestdogstuff.com

Second Developmental Deadline
(Before You Select Your Puppy)

Evaluating Your Prospective Puppy's Progress

By the time you bring your new puppy home, say at eight weeks of age, it should already be accustomed to an indoor domestic environment (especially one with noises) and well-socialized with people. Similarly, housetraining, chewtoy-training, and tutoring in basic manners should be well underway. If not, your prospective puppy's social and mental development is already severely retarded, and sadly you will be playing catch-up for the rest of its life. Your puppy will require remedial socialization and training for a long time to come.

Make absolutely certain that your prospective puppy has been raised indoors in close contact with people who have devoted lots of time to its education.

If a dog is expected to live in a household with people, obviously it needs to have been raised in a household with people. Your puppy needs to be prepared for the clamor of everyday domestic living: the noise of the vacuum cleaner, pots and pans dropping in the kitchen, sports programs screaming on the television, children crying, and adults arguing. Exposure to such stimuli while its eyes and ears are still developing allows the puppy (with blurred vision and muffled hearing) to

BEFORE YOU GET YOUR PUPPY

gradually become accustomed to sights and sounds that might otherwise frighten it when older.

There is not much point in choosing a puppy that has been raised in the relative social isolation of a backyard, basement, barn, garage, or kennel, where there is precious little opportunity for interaction with people and a puppy has become accustomed to soiling its living area and yapping a lot. Puppies raised in physical seclusion and partial social isolation are hardly prepared for household living, and they are certainly not prepared for encounters with children or men. Backyard- and kennel-raised puppies are certainly not pet-quality dogs; they are livestock on par with veal calves and battery hens. Look elsewhere! Look for litters which have been born and raised in a kitchen or living room.

If you want a companion dog to share your home, it obviously should have been raised in a home, not a cage.

How to Select a Good Puppy

Your prospective puppy should feel thoroughly at ease being handled by strangers (i.e., by you and your family). The puppy should be fully desensitized to sounds before it is four weeks old. Likewise, its housetraining program should be well underway, its favorite toy should be a chewtoy (stuffed with puppy chow), and it should happily and eagerly come, follow, sit, lie down, and roll over when requested. If these are not so, either your puppy is a slow learner or it has had a poor teacher. In either case, look elsewhere.

An essential ingredient of puppy husbandry is regular (several times a day) handling, gentling, and calming by a wide variety of people, especially children, men, and strangers. These exercises are especially important during the early weeks and especially with those breeds which are notoriously tricky when handled by strangers—that is, several Asian breeds, plus many herding, working, and terrier breeds, i.e., most breeds of dog!

The second most important quality in any dog is that it enjoys interacting with people, specifically that it enjoys being handled by all people, especially children, men, and strangers. Early socialization easily prevents serious adult problems.

The single most important quality for a dog is developing bite inhibition and a soft mouth during puppyhood.

Handling and Gentling

If you want a cuddly adult dog, it needs to have been cuddled on a regular basis as a puppy. Certainly, neonatal pups are pretty fragile and helpless critters; they can barely walk and they have a number of sensory constraints. But they still need to be socialized. Neonatal pups are extremely sensitive and impressionable, and this is the very best time to accustom them to being handled. Neonatal puppies may not see or hear very well, but they can smell and feel. Neonatal and early puppy socialization, being of paramount importance, must be done gently and carefully.

- Ask the breeder how many people have handled, gentled, trained, and played with the pups daily.
- Specifically, ask the breeder how many children, men, and strangers have worked with the puppies.
- Handle each puppy to see how it enjoys being cuddled (gently restrained); specifically, see how it enjoys being stroked and massaged (examined) around its neck, muzzle, ears, paws, and rear end.

Alpha Rollovers???

Trainers from The Dark Side suggest grabbing a young pup by the cheeks, flipping it onto its back and forcibly holding it down to see if it struggles. They call this procedure the Alpha Rollover. It is as stupid as it is cruel. How would you feel if a dog weighing 2000 pounds unexpectedly grabbed you by the scruff and stared menacingly into your eyes? If you didn't struggle, you would most probably go limp out of fear and wet your pants. All this silly maneuver proves is that puppies are scared when people frighten them and that, of course, scared puppies either struggle or go limp.

Certainly you need to determine how readily your potential pup accepts and enjoys handling and restraint, but it is not necessary to frighten the living daylights out of it. Simply pick up the puppy and gently cuddle it in your arms. You'll soon find out whether it relaxes like a ragdoll or kicks and struggles. If it struggles, hold on gently while you soothingly stroke it between the eyes or massage its ears or chest, and see how quickly you can calm it down.

Sound Sensitivity

Exposure to a variety of sounds should commence well before the eyes and ears are fully opened, especially with sound-sensitive dogs, e.g., herding and obedience breeds.

It is quite normal for puppies to react to noises. What you are trying to evaluate is the level of each pup's reaction and bounce-back time. For example, we expect a puppy to react to a sudden and unexpected loud noise, but we do not expect it to go to pieces or experience a lengthy reaction. Judge whether the puppy reacts or overreacts to sounds, and time how long it takes for the puppy to approach and take a food treat (the bounce-back time). Expect immeasurably short bounce-back times from bull breeds, and short bounce-backs from working dogs and terriers, but be prepared for longer bounce-back times from toys and herding breeds. However, regardless of a dog's breed or type, excessive overreaction, panic, or extremely lengthy bounce-back times are all proof of insufficient socialization. Unless successfully rehabilitated, such pups may become extremely reactive and difficult to live with when grown-up.

- Ask the breeder about the extent of the litter's exposure to domestic noise. Are the puppies being raised indoors?
- Specifically, ask the breeder whether or not the puppies have been exposed to loud and unexpected noises, such as adults shouting, children crying, television (male voices shouting and screaming on ESPN), radio, and music (C&W, Rock, and Classical—Tchaikovsky's 1812 Overture).
- Evaluate the puppies' response to a variety of noises, for example, people taking, laughing, crying, and shouting, a whistle, a hiss, or a single hand clap.

Household Etiquette

Ask the breeder about the litter's ongoing errorless housetraining and chewtoy training program. Try to observe the litter for at least an hour and pay attention to what each puppy chews and where each puppy relieves itself.

If the puppies have no available toilet and the entire puppy area has been covered with sheets of newspaper, the puppies will have developed a strong preference for going on paper and will need specialized housetraining in their new home. Moreover, if there is no toilet and the entire area has been littered with straw or shredded paper, the puppies will have learned they may eliminate anywhere and everywhere, which is what they will do in your home. The older the puppy raised in these conditions, the more difficult it will be to housetrain.

- Check for the use of several hollow chewtoys (such as Kongs, Biscuit Balls, and sterilized bones) stuffed with kibble.
- Check for the use of a doggy toilet in the puppies' living area. Estimating how many piles and puddles are in the toilet versus on the floor will offer a good indication of where the puppy will eliminate when it comes to your home.

Basic Manners

Inquire about the litter's ongoing obedience training program and ask the breeder to demonstrate the puppies' basic obedience skills, for example, to come, sit, lie down, and roll over.

- Evaluate each puppy's response to your lure/reward training attempts using pieces of kibble and a Kong as lures and rewards.

Personal Preference

When choosing the puppy, it is so important that all family members agree. You want to select the puppy that you all like the best, and you want to select a puppy who likes all of you. Sit down quietly as a family and see which puppies make contact first and which ones stay around the longest.

For years it was dogmatically stated that puppies which approached quickly, jumped-up, and bit your hands were totally unsuitable as pets, since they were aggressive and difficult to train. On the contrary, these are normal, well-socialized, eight-

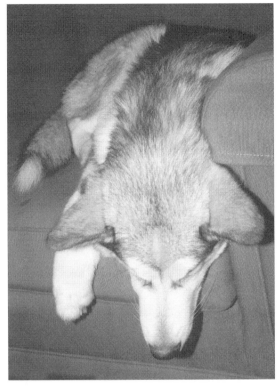

Spend at least two hours when selecting a puppy. Eight-week-old pups cycle between extreme hyperactivity and total exhaustion every ninety minutes or so. Make sure you get a comprehensive impression of the puppy's total behavior repertoire.

week-old puppies who are simply saying hello in true puppy fashion without the benefit of manners. With some very basic training to redirect the pup's delightful exuberance, you'll have the fastest recalls and the quickest sits in puppy class. Also, puppy biting is both normal and absolutely necessary. In fact the more dogs bite as puppies, the softer and safer their jaws in adulthood. (For more information about bite inhibition, please see *AFTER You Get Your Puppy,* or *Preventing Aggression.*)

I would be more concerned about puppies that were slow to approach or remained in hiding. It is completely, utterly, and absolutely abnormal for a well-socialized six- to eight-week-old puppy to be shy when approaching people. If the puppy acts shy or scared, then without a doubt it has not been sufficiently socialized. Look elsewhere. If, however, you really have your heart set on taking a shy puppy, only do so if each family member can coax the pup to approach and take a food treat. A shy puppy represents a substantial time commitment, since it will need to be hand-fed kibble every day from a variety of strangers. To rehabilitate this pup, you'll certainly have your work cut out for you during the next four weeks

Beware of breeders who want to force their choice on you about raising your pup for conformation shows and not having it neutered. Remember, the puppy is coming to live with you. Raising the pup is your responsibility, and decisions regarding its show career and reproductive status are yours to make.

There are numerous wonderful activities that you can enjoy with your neutered dog, including competitive, rally, and freestyle obedience, agility, carting, flyball, Frisbee, K9 Games, search and rescue, sledding, tracking, and of course, dog walks and trips to the dog park.

It's entirely your choice, but please neuter your puppy. Each year, millions of puppies and young adult dogs are euthanized (killed) in animal shelters. It's simply not fair for puppies, and it is not fair for animal-loving shelter personnel. Please don't add to the numbers. Please neuter your puppy.

Singleton Puppies

Most pups have adequate opportunity to play with their littermates during their first eight weeks. Singleton and hand-reared pups have had insufficient opportunity to play (play-fight and play-bite) and therefore, teaching bite inhibition is a top priority. Enroll in a puppy classes as soon as your puppy reaches three months of age. Play and socialization are essential for puppies to develop and maintain a soft mouth.

Common Pitfalls

"Our last dog was perfectly trustworthy."
Maybe you were just lucky and picked a born-to-be-perfect puppy. Or maybe you were an excellent trainer. But can you still remember what you did back then and do you still have the time to do it?

"Our last dog just loved kids!"
A young family doted on their first dog and devoted a lot of time to its training. The whole family attended puppy classes and held puppy parties at home for the children's friends. So many children spent time playing games and reward-training the dog that of course the dog loved children. The dog enjoyed its sunset years proudly watching the children grow up and graduate from high school. By the time the parents got their second dog, the children had all left the nest. The new puppy grows up in a world without children. All is well for many years—that is, until grandchildren appear on the scene.

If You Really Want a Housetraining Challenge

If you really want to set yourself a housetraining challenge, buy a three-month-old puppy from a pet store window that is littered with shredded paper and straw and has no specific toilet area. This puppy has been trained to eliminate anywhere, anytime. And that's exactly what it will do when you get it home. You'll be cleaning up urine and feces for a very long time!

Remember

You are choosing a pup to come and live in your home and adapt to your lifestyle, so please make sure the puppy has been prepared for domestic life in general and is suitable for your lifestyle in particular. Beware of statements like:

"We haven't taught the puppies to sit because they are showdogs."
Basically this breeder is under the impression the dog is so dumb it can not tell the difference between two simple instructions such as "Sit" and "Stand." Look elsewhere. Just because the breeder is prepared to live with dogs that haven't even been taught to sit does not mean to say you should! Also, if the puppy hasn't even been taught basic manners, there are probably many other things the breeder failed to teach.

"He's the scaredy-cat of the litter."
Certainly, in any litter individual dogs will display different tendencies to approach strangers (you), but no eight-week-old puppy should be scared to approach people. Any shyness, fearfulness, or tendency to avoid people should have been noticed and dealt with as early as four weeks ago. The shy puppy should have been supersocialized. A single scaredy-cat puppy in a litter indicates that the breeder has not been vigilant in assessing day-to-day socialization. There are most probably other good puppies in the litter, but I suggest that you be vigilant when assessing their socialization status.

Third Developmental Deadline
(The First Day Your Puppy Comes Home)

Errorless Housetraining and Chewtoy-Training

What to Teach Your Puppy During its First Week at Home

Your canine newcomer is just itching to learn domestic household manners. It wants to please, but it has to know *how* to please. Before the young pup can be trusted to have full run of the house, somebody must teach the house rules. There's no point keeping house rules a secret. Somebody has to tell the pup, and that somebody is you. Otherwise, your puppy will let its imagination run wild in its quest for occupational therapy to pass the time of day. Without a firm grounding in canine domestic etiquette, your puppy will be left to improvise in his choice of toys and toilets. The pup will no doubt eliminate in closets and on carpets, and your couches and curtains will be viewed as mere playthings for destruction. If your pup is allowed to make "mistakes," bad habits will quickly become the accepted status quo. Then it becomes necessary to break bad habits before teaching good habits.

Your puppy's living quarters need to be designed so that housetraining and chewtoy training are errorless. Each mistake is a potential disaster, since it heralds many more to come.

Errorless Housetraining and Chewtoy-Training

Successful domestic doggy education involves teaching your puppy to train itself via confinement so as to prevent mistakes and establish good habits from the outset. When you are physically or mentally absent, confine your puppy to keep him out of mischief and to help him learn how to act appropriately.

The more you confine your puppy to its Doggy Den and Puppy Playroom during its first few weeks at home, the more freedom it will enjoy as an adult dog for the rest of its life. The more closely you follow the following puppy-confinement program, the sooner your puppy will be housetrained and chewtoy trained. And, as an added benefit, your puppy will learn to settle down quickly, quietly, calmly, and happily.

When You Are Not at Home

Keep your puppy confined to a fairly small puppy playroom (long-term confinement area), such as the kitchen, bathroom, or a utility room. Maybe use an exercise pen to cordon off a small section of a room. Your puppy's long-term confinement area should include:

1. A comfortable bed
2. A bowl of fresh water
3. Plenty of hollow chewtoys (stuffed with dog food)
4. A doggy toilet in the farthest corner from its bed

Obviously, your puppy will feel the need to bark, chew, and eliminate throughout the course of the day, and so he must be left somewhere he can satisfy his needs without causing any damage or annoyance. Your puppy will most probably eliminate as far as possible from his sleeping quarters, i.e., in his doggy toilet. By removing all chewable items from the puppy playpen with the exception of hollow chewtoys stuffed with kibble, you will make chewing chewtoys your puppy's favorite habit—a good habit! Long-term confinement allows your puppy to teach itself to use an appropriate dog toilet, to want to chew appropriate chewtoys, and to settle down quietly.

When you are not at home, confine your puppy to a playroom which has a comfortable bed, a bowl of water, stuffed chewtoys, and a toilet.

The purpose of long-term confinement is twofold:
1. To confine the puppy to an area where chewing and toilet behavior is acceptable, so the puppy does not make any chewing or housesoiling mistakes around the house
2. To maximize the likelihood that the puppy will learn to use the provided toilet, to chew only chewtoys (the only chewables available in the playroom), and to settle down calmly without barking

When You Are at Home

Enjoy short play and training sessions hourly. If you can not pay full attention to your puppy every single second, play with your pup in his Puppy Playpen, where a suitable toilet and toys are available. Otherwise, for periods of no longer than an hour at a time, confine your puppy to his Doggy Den (short-term close confinement area), such as a portable dog crate. Every hour, release your puppy and quickly take it to its doggy toilet. Your puppy's short-term confinement area should include a comfortable bed, and plenty of hollow chewtoys (stuffed with dog food).

It is much easier to watch your pup if he is settled down in a single spot. Either you may move the crate so that your puppy is in the same room as you, or you may want to confine your pup to a different room to start preparing him for times when he will be left at home alone. If you do not like the idea of confining your puppy to a dog crate, you may tie the leash to your belt and have the pup settle down at your feet. Or you may fasten the leash to an eye-hook in the baseboard next to your puppy's bed, basket, or mat. To prevent the chewtoys from rolling out of reach, also tie them to the eye-hook.

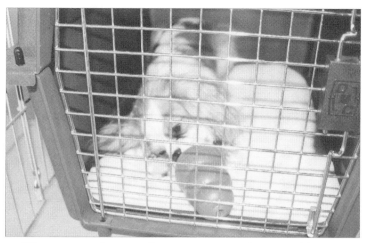

When you are at home, confine your puppy to a dog crate with some stuffed chewtoys. Every hour take your puppy to an appropriate toilet area and it will eliminate within seconds (two minutes max.).

The purpose of short-term close confinement is threefold:

1. To confine the puppy to an area where chewing behavior is acceptable, so the puppy does not make chewing mistakes around the house

2. To make the puppy a chewtoyaholic (since chewtoys are the only chewables available and they are stuffed with food) and to teach the puppy to settle down calmly and happily for periodic quiet moments

3. To prevent housesoiling mistakes around the house *and to predict when the puppy needs to eliminate.* Closely confining a puppy to its bed strongly inhibits urination and defecation, so the pup will need to relieve itself when released from the crate each hour. The owner will then be there to show the puppy the right spot, reward it for eliminating in the right spot, and then enjoy a short play/training session with the delightfully empty puppy.

Most dog crates are portable and may easily be moved from room to room so that when you are at home, your puppy learns to settle down quickly and amuse itself quietly. Then you can settle down and amuse yourself and read a book in the living room...

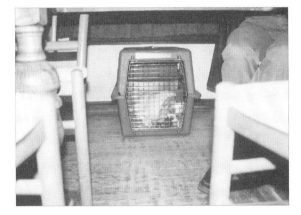

...eat dinner in the dining room...

...or work at the computer.

Train Your Puppy to Train Itself

Housetraining and chewtoy training will be quick and easy if you adhere to the above puppy confinement plan, which prevents the puppy from making any mistakes and prompts the puppy to teach itself household etiquette. If you vary from the program you will likely experience problems. Unless you enjoy problems, you must reprimand yourself for any mistake you allow your puppy to make.

Errorless Housetraining

Housesoiling is a spatial problem, involving perfectly normal, natural, and necessary canine behaviors (peeing and pooping) performed in inappropriate places.

Housetraining is quickly and easily accomplished by praising your puppy and offering a food treat when it eliminates in an appropriate toilet area. Once your pup realizes that its eliminatory products are the equivalent of coins in a food vending machine (i.e., that feces and urine may be cashed in for tasty treats), your pup will want to eliminate in the appropriate spot, because soiling the house does not bring equivalent fringe benefits.

Housesoiling is also a temporal problem: either the puppy is in the wrong place at the right time (i.e., confined indoors with full bladder and bowels), or the puppy is in the right place at the wrong time (i.e., outdoors in the yard or on a walk, but with empty bladder and bowels).

Timing is the essence of successful housetraining. Indeed, efficient and effective housetraining depends upon the owner being able to predict when the puppy needs to eliminate so that it may be directed to an appropriate toilet area and more than adequately rewarded for doing the right thing in the right place at the right time.

Usually, puppies urinate within half a minute of waking up from a nap and they usually defecate within a couple of minutes. But who has the time to hang around to wait for puppy to wake up and pee and poop? Instead it's a better plan to wake up the puppy yourself, when you are ready and the time is right.

Short-term confinement offers a convenient means to accurately predict when your puppy needs to relieve itself. Confining a pup to a small area strongly inhibits it from urinating or defecating, since it doesn't want to soil his sleeping area. Hence, the puppy is highly likely to want to eliminate immediately after being released from confinement.

Housetraining Is as Easy as 1-2-3

When you are away from home or if you are too busy or distracted to adhere to the following schedule, keep your puppy confined to its puppy playroom where it has a suitable doggy toilet. Otherwise, when you are at home:

1. Keep your puppy closely confined to its doggy den (crate) or on-leash
2. Every hour on the hour release your pup from confinement and quickly run it (on-leash if necessary) to the toilet area, instruct your pup to eliminate, and give it three minutes to do so
3. Enthusiastically praise your puppy when it eliminates, offer three freeze-dried liver treats, and then play/train with the pup indoors; once your puppy is old enough to go outside, take it for a walk after it eliminates

Errorless housetraining is so simple and so effective. Why do so many dog owners experience problems?

Why confine the pup to its doggy den; why not its playroom?
Short-term close confinement allows you to predict when your puppy wants to go so that you may be there to direct it to the appropriate spot and reward it for doing the right thing in the right place at the right time. During the hour-long periods of close confinement, as your puppy lies doggo in dreamy repose, its bladder and bowels are slowly but surely filling up, such that whenever the big hand reaches twelve and you dutifully release the pup to run to its indoor toilet or backyard doggy toilet to relieve itself, your puppy is likely to eliminate pronto. Knowing when your puppy wants to go allows you to choose the spot and most importantly to reward your puppy handsomely for using it. Rewarding your puppy for using its toilet is the secret to successful housetraining. If, on the other hand the puppy were left in its playroom, it would most likely use its indoor toilet but would not be rewarded for doing so.

What if my puppy doesn't like going in its crate?
Before confining your puppy to its crate (doggy den), you first need to teach it to love the crate and to love confinement. This is so easy to do. Stuff a couple of hollow chewtoys with kibble and the occasional treat. Let your puppy sniff the stuffed chewtoys and then place them in the crate and shut the door with your puppy on the outside. Usually it takes just a few seconds for your puppy to beg you to open the door and let it inside and in no time at all, your pup will be happily preoccupied with its chewtoys.

When leaving the puppy in its long-term confinement area, tie the stuffed chewtoys to the inside of the crate and leave the

Before confining your puppy, make sure that it enjoys spending time in its crate. Feeding all of its dinner kibble stuffed into Kongs inside its crate usually does the trick within a couple of days. The following technique works even quicker. Have your puppy sit while you open the crate door...

...place a stuffed Kong inside the crate and close the door...

...with your puppy on the outside! Let the pup dwell on its dilemma—stuffed Kong inside and puppy locked outside—and then after a while, open the crate door...

66

crate door open. Thus, the puppy can choose whether it wants to explore the small area or lie down on its bed in its crate and try to extricate the kibble and treats from its chewtoys. Basically, the stuffed chewtoys are confined to the crate and the puppy is given the option of coming or going at will. Most puppies choose to rest comfortably inside the crate with stuffed chewtoys for entertainment. This techniques works especially well if your puppy is not fed kibble from a bowl but only from chewtoys or by hand (as lures and rewards in training).

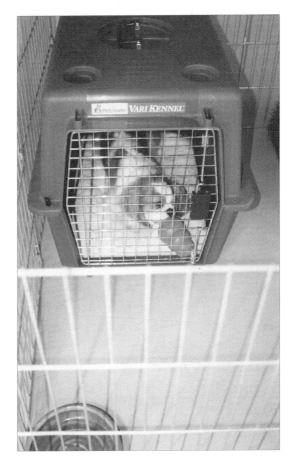

...and your puppy will eagerly dash inside the crate and quickly settle down to chew its chewtoy.

What if I don't like putting my puppy in a crate?

Short-term confinement (whether to a crate or tie-down) is a temporary training measure to help you teach your puppy where to eliminate (in its doggy toilet) and what to chew (chewtoys stuffed with kibble and treats). A dog crate is the best housetraining tool to help you accurately predict when your dog wishes to relieve itself and is the best training tool to help you to teach your puppy to become a chewtoyaholic. Once your puppy has learned to eliminate only in appropriate areas and to chew only appropriate objects, it may be given free run of the house and garden for the rest of its life. You will probably find however, that after just a few days your puppy learns to love its crate and will voluntarily rest inside. Your puppy's very own den is a quiet, comfortable, and special doggy place.

If, on the other hand, your puppy is given unsupervised free run of the house from the outset, the odds are that it will be confined later on—first to the yard, then to the basement, then to a cage in an animal shelter, and then to a coffin. Without a doubt, housesoiling and destructive chewing are the two most prevalent terminal illnesses in dogs. Using a dog crate will help you prevent these problems from ever developing in your puppy.

Why not just leave the puppy outdoors until it is housetrained?

Who is going to housetrain your pup outside—a shrub? If the dog is left outside unattended, it will become an indiscriminate eliminator. Basically, your puppy will learn to go wherever it wants, whenever it wants, and it will likely do the same whenever you let it indoors. Puppies left outdoors and unsupervised for long periods of time seldom become housetrained. Also, they tend to become indiscriminate barkers, chewers, diggers, and escapists, and they may more easily be stolen. Outdoor puppies become so excited on the few occasions they are invited indoors that eventually they are no longer allowed inside at all.

Why release the pup every hour; why not every 55 minutes, or every three hours? And is it really necessary to do it on the hour? Puppies have a 45-minute bladder capacity at three weeks of age, 75-minute capacity at eight weeks, 90-minute capacity at twelve weeks and two-hour capacity at 18 weeks. Releasing your puppy every hour offers you an hourly opportunity to reward your dog for using a designated toilet area. You do not have to do this precisely each hour, but it is much easier to remember to do so each hour on the hour.

Why run the puppy to the toilet; why not walk sedately?
If you take your time getting your puppy to its doggy toilet, you may find that it pees or poops en route. Hurrying your puppy tends to jiggle its bowels and bladder so that it really wants to go the moment you let it stand still and sniff its toilet area.

Why not just put the puppy outside; can't it do it on its own?
Of course it can. But the whole point of predicting when your puppy wants to relieve itself is so you may be there to show it where and to offer well-deserved praise and rewards. Thus your puppy will learn where you would like it to go. Also, if you see your puppy eliminate, you know that it is empty; you may then allow your empty puppy supervised exploration of the house for a while before returning it to its den.

Why instruct the pup to eliminate; doesn't he know he wants to go?
By instructing your puppy to eliminate beforehand and by rewarding it for eliminating afterwards you will teach your pup

to go on command. Eliminating on cue is a boon when you are travelling with your dog and in other situations when there is only a short time for potty breaks. Ask your pup to "Hurry up," "Do your business," or "Go Pee and Poop," or use some other socially acceptable, euphemistic eliminatory command.

Why give the puppy three minutes; isn't one minute sufficient?
Usually, a young pup will urinate within 30 seconds of being released from short-term close confinement, but it may take one or two minutes for it to defecate. It is certainly worthwhile allowing your pup three minutes to complete its business

What if the puppy doesn't go?
Your puppy will be more likely to eliminate if you stand still and let it circle around you on leash. If your puppy does not eliminate within the allotted time, no biggie! Simply pop the pup back in its crate and try again in half an hour. Repeat the process over and over until it does eliminate. Eventually, your puppy will eliminate outdoors and you will be able to reward it. Therefore, on subsequent hourly trips to its toilet your puppy will be likely to eliminate promptly.

Why praise the puppy; isn't relief sufficient reward?
It is far better to express your emotions when praising your puppy for getting it right, than when reprimanding the poor pup for getting it wrong. So *really praise that pup:* "Gooooooooood Puppy!" Housetraining is no time for understated thank yous. Don't be embarrassed about praising your puppy. Embarrassed dog owners usually end up with housesoiling problems. Really reward your puppy. Tell your puppy that it has done *a most wonderful and glorious thing!*

Why offer treats; isn't praise sufficient reward?
In a word, no! The average person cannot effectively praise a sick lettuce. And specifically, many owners (especially men) seem to be incapable of convincingly praising their puppies. Consequently, it might be a good idea to give the pup a food treat or two (or three) for its effort. Input for output! "Wow! My owner's great; every time I pee or poop outside, she gives me a treat. I never get yummy treats when I do it on the couch. I can't wait for my owner to come home so I can go out in the yard and cash in my urine and feces for food treats!" In fact, why not keep some treats in a screw-top jar handy to the doggy toilet?

Why freeze-dried liver?
Housetraining is one of those times when you want to pull out all of the stops. Take my word for it: When it comes to housetraining, use the Ferrari of dog treats—freeze-dried liver.

Do we really have to give three liver treats when the puppy pees or poops; isn't this a wee bit anal retentive?
Yes and no. Certainly you do not have to give your puppy exactly three treats every time. But it's a funny thing: If I suggest that people offer a treat each time their puppy eliminates promptly in the right place, they rarely follow instructions. However, whenever I tell people to give three treats, they will painstakingly count out the treats to give to their puppy. What I am trying to say is: Handsomely praise and reward your puppy *every* time it uses a designated toilet area.

Why play with the puppy indoors?
If you reward your pup for using its doggy toilet, you will know it is empty. "Thank you, empty puppy!" What better time to play with or train your puppy indoors without entertaining the

risk of a messy mistake. Why get a puppy unless you want to spend some quality (feces-free) time with it?

Why bother to take an older puppy outdoors for a walk when it's empty?
Many people fall into the trap of taking their puppy outside or walking it so that it may eliminate, and when it does they bring it indoors. Usually it takes just a couple of trials before the puppy learns, "Whenever my urine or feces hits the ground, my walk ends!" Consequently, the pup becomes reluctant to eliminate outside, and so when brought home after a long jiggling play or walk, it is in dire need to relieve itself. Which it does. It is a much better plan to praise your puppy for using its doggy toilet and then take it for a walk as a reward for eliminating.

Get in the habit of taking an older puppy to its doggy toilet (in your yard or curbside in front of your apartment building), standing still, and waiting for the pup to eliminate. Praise the pup and offer liver treats when it does: "Good dog, let's go walkies!" Clean up and dispose of the feces in your own trash can, and then go and enjoy a poopless walk with your dog. After just a few days with a simple "no poop-no walk" rule, you'll find you have the quickest urinator and defecator in town.

What should I do if I've done all the above and I catch the puppy in the act of making a mistake?
Pick up a rolled newspaper and give yourself a smack! Obviously you did not follow the instructions above. Who allowed the urine-and-feces-full puppy to have free-range access to your house? You! Should you ever reprimand or punish your puppy when you catch it in the act, all it will learn is to eliminate in secret—that is, never again in your

untrustworthy presence. Thus you will have created an owner-absent housesoiling problem. If you ever catch your pup in the act of making a mistake that was your fault, at the very most you can quickly, softly, but urgently implore your pup, "Outside, outside, outside!" The tone and urgency of your voice communicates that you want your puppy to do something promptly, and the meaning of the words instruct the puppy where. Your response will have limited effect on the present mistake, but it helps prevent future mistakes.

Never reprimand your dog in a manner which is not instructive. Nonspecific reprimands only create more problems (owner-absent misbehavior) as well as frightening the pup and eroding the puppy-owner relationship. Your puppy is not a "bad puppy." On the contrary, your puppy is a good puppy who has been forced to misbehave because its owner could not, or would not, follow simple instructions.

Please reread and follow the above instructions!

Every hour on the hour, take your puppy to its toilet area (either its permanent toilet in the yard or the temporary toilet in its long-term confinement area), and handsomely reward the pup as soon as it eliminates.

Doggy Toilet

For the best doggy toilet, equip the litter box (or cover a piece of old linoleum) with what will be the dog's eventual toilet substrate. For example, for rural and suburban pups who will eventually be taught to relieve themselves outside on earth or grass, lay down a roll of turf. For urban puppies who will eventually be taught to eliminate at curbside, lay down a couple of thin concrete tiles. Your puppy will soon develop a very strong natural preference for eliminating on similar outdoor surfaces whenever it can.

If you have a backyard, besides having an indoor toilet in your pup's playroom, take it to its outdoor toilet in the yard whenever you release it from its doggy den. If you live in an apartment and do not have a yard, teach your puppy to use its indoor toilet until it is old enough to venture outdoors (three months of age).

Training Your Dog to Use an Outdoor Toilet

For the first few weeks, take your puppy outside on-leash. Hurry to its toilet area and then *stand still* to allow the puppy to circle (as it would normally do before eliminating). Reward your puppy each time it "goes" in the designated spot. If you have a fenced yard, you may later take your puppy outside off-leash and let it choose where it would like to eliminate. But make sure to reward it differentially according to how close it hits ground zero. Offer one treat for doing it outside quickly, two treats for doing it within, say, five yards of the doggy toilet, three treats for within two yards, and five treats for a bull's eye.

Problems

If you're having problems with housesoiling or house destruction after one week, consult the *Housetraining* and *Chewing* Behavior Booklets.

Errorless Chewtoy-Training

The dog is a social and inquisitive animal. It needs to do something, especially if left at home alone. What would you like your dog to do? Crosswords? Needlepoint? Watch soaps on the telly? You must provide some form of occupational therapy for your puppy to pass the time of day. If your puppy learns to enjoy chewing chewtoys, it will look forward to settling down quietly for some quality chewing-time. It is important to teach your puppy to enjoy chewing chewtoys more than chewing household items. An effective ploy is to stuff the puppy's chewtoys with kibble and treats. In fact, during your puppy's first few weeks at home, put away its food bowl and (apart from kibble used as lures and rewards for training), *only* serve your puppy's kibble stuffed in hollow chewtoys, e.g., Kongs, Biscuit Balls, and sterilized bones.

For errorless chewtoy-training, adhere to the puppy confinement program. When you are away from home, leave the puppy in its puppy playroom with bed, water, toilet, and plenty of stuffed chewtoys. When you are at home, leave the puppy in its doggy den with plenty of stuffed chewtoys. Every hour after releasing the pup to relieve itself, play chewtoy games—chewtoy-search, chewtoy-fetch, and chewtoy-tug-o'-war. Your puppy will soon develop a very strong chewtoy habit because you have limited its chewing choices to a single acceptable toy, which you have made even more attractive with the addition of kibble and treats.

Once your dog has become a chewtoyaholic and has not had a chewing (or housesoiling) mishap for at least three months, you may increase your puppy's playroom to two rooms. For each subsequent month without a mistake your puppy may gain access to another room, until eventually it enjoys free run of the entire house and garden when left at home alone. If a chewing mistake should occur, go back to the original puppy confinement program for at least a month.

In addition to preventing household destruction, teaching your puppy to become a chewtoyaholic prevents it from

During its first couple of weeks at home, unless you are training or playing with your puppy, make sure it spends all of its time in its long-term or short-term confinement area, where the only available chewable objects are chewtoys stuffed with kibble and the occasional treat.

becoming a recreational barker because chewing and barking are mutually exclusive behaviors. Also, chewtoyaholism helps your puppy learn to settle down calmly because chewing and dashing about are mutually exclusive behaviors.

Chewtoyaholism is especially useful for dogs with Obsessive-Compulsive Disorder since it provides them with an acceptable and convenient means to work out their obsessions and compulsions. Your dog may still have OCD, but if it is a chewtoyaholic it will happily spend its time obsessively and compulsively chewing its stuffed chewtoys.

And most importantly, chewtoy chewing keeps the puppy occupied and effectively helps prevent the development of separation anxiety.

What Is a Chewtoy?

A chewtoy is an object for the dog to chew which is neither destructible nor consumable. If your dog destroys an object, you will have to replace it, and that costs money. If your dog consumes the object, you may have to replace your dog. Eating non-food items is extremely hazardous to your dog's health.

The type of chewtoy you choose will depend on your dog's penchant for chewing and its individual preferences. I have seen some dogs make a cow's hoof or a compressed rawhide chewy last forever, whereas other dogs consume them in a matter of minutes. Personally, I think Kong products are the Cadillacs of chewtoys. Hollow sterilized long bones are a very close second choice. I like Kong products and sterilized bones because they are simple, natural, and organic (not plastic). Also, being hollow, they may be stuffed with food. Kong products and sterilized bones are obtainable from any good pet supply store.

Dinner from Chewtoys, Not from Bowls

Customarily, puppies receive their entire daily allotment of kibble at dinner, which often becomes a jackpot reward for boisterously barking and expectantly bouncing around. Moreover, if you allow your puppy to wolf down dinner from a bowl, it will be at a loss for what to do for the rest of the day. In the wild, dogs spend a good 90 percent of their waking hours searching for food, so in a sense, regular bowl-feeding deprives a dog of its principal activity—searching for food. Instead your inquisitive puppy will search for entertainment all day long, and most likely you will consider your puppy's choices of occupation to be mischievous misbehavior.

Without a doubt, regularly feeding a new puppy (or adult dog) from a bowl is the single most disastrous mistake in dog husbandry and training. Although unintentional, the effects of bowl-feeding are often severely detrimental for the puppy's household manners and sense of well-being. In a sense, each bowl-fed meal steals the puppy's *raison d'etre,* its very reason for being. Within seconds of gulping its meal, the poor pup now faces a mental void for the rest of its day with nothing but long, lonely hours to worry and fret, or work itself into a frenzy.

As the puppy adapts to fill the void, normal behaviors such as chewing, barking, strolling, grooming, and playing become stereotypical, repetitive, and maladaptive. Specific behaviors increase in frequency until they no longer serve any useful function except to pass the time. Investigative chewing becomes destructive chewing. Alarm barking becomes incessant barking. Strolling from one place to another becomes repetitively pacing or racing back and forth. Investigating a

Squeaky toys are very effective lures and rewards in training, but... a squeaky toy is not a suitable chewtoy! Squeaky toys are both destructible and consumable. Allowing a young pup unsupervised play with intriguing and easily destroyed items will turn it into a destructive chewer in no time at all.

Chewtoys should be virtually indestructible, made of natural products (such as rubber or bone), and hollow (stuffable). Stuffing chewtoys with kibble and the occasional treat encourages the pup to focus on extricating the food, rather than on destroying the toy. Stuffing chewtoys prolongs their life expectancy. The very best chewtoys are Kongs, Biscuit Balls, and sterilized bones.

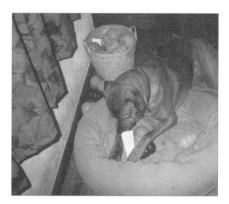

Once your dog has learned that designated chewtoys are the only appropriate chewtoys, it may be trusted to retrieve, or play with other items. Ivan had a footwear fetish; he loved retrieving slippers and shoes, carrying slippers and shoes, and snuggling and sleeping with slippers and shoes. But he never destroyed them, and he could always find them when they were misplaced.

shadow or light becomes a neurotic fixation. Routine grooming becomes excessive licking, scratching, tail-chasing, head-pressing, or in extreme cases, self-mutilation.

Stereotyped behaviors cause the release of endorphins, perpetuating their repetition, and in a sense, the dog becomes drugged and hooked on mindless, repetitive activity. Stereotyped behaviors are like behavioral cancers; as they progressively increase in frequency and squeeze most useful and adaptive responses from the dog's behavior repertoire until eventually the "brain-dead" dog spends hours on end barking, pacing, chewing itself, or simply staring into space.

A vital facet of your puppy's early education is to teach it how to peacefully pass the time of day. Feeding your puppy's kibble only from hollow chewtoys—Kongs, Biscuit Balls and sterilized bones—keeps your puppy happily occupied and content for hours on end. It allows the puppy to focus on an enjoyable activity so that it doesn't dwell on its loneliness. Each piece of extracted kibble also rewards your puppy for settling down calmly, for chewing an appropriate chewtoy, and for not barking.

Chewtoy Stuffing

An old chewtoy becomes immediately novel and exciting when stuffed with food. If you use kibble from your puppy's normal daily ration your puppy will not put on weight. To protect your puppy's waistline, heart, and liver, it is important to minimize the use of treats in training. Use kibble as lures and rewards for teaching basic manners and reserve freeze-dried liver treats for initial housetraining, for meeting children, men, and strangers, as a garnish for stuffing Kongs (see below), and as an occasional jackpot reward for especially good behavior.

Kong Stuffing 101

The basic principle of Kong stuffing ensures that some food comes out quickly and easily to instantly reward your puppy for initially contacting its chewtoy; bits of food come out over a long period of time to periodically reward your puppy for continuing to chew; and some of the best bits never come out, so your puppy never loses interest. Squish a small piece of freeze-dried liver in the small hole in the Kong: this your puppy will never be able to get out. Smear a little honey around the inside of the Kong, fill it up with kibble, and then block the big hole with crossed MilkBones.

There are numerous creative variations on basic Kong stuffing. One of my favorite recipes comprises moistening your puppy's kibble, spooning it into the Kong, and then putting it in the freezer overnight—a Kongsicle! Your dog will love it.

Kong is King!

If from the outset you always confine your puppy with a selection of stuffed Kongs and Biscuit Balls, chewing these appropriate chewtoys will soon become an integral part of its day. Your puppy will quickly develop a socially acceptable Kong habit. And remember, good habits are just as hard to break as bad

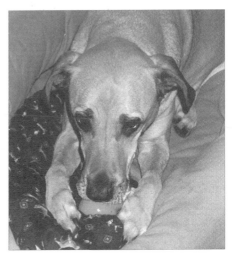

habits. Your puppy will now spend a large part of its day musing over its Kong products.

Let's pause for a moment to consider all the bad things your puppy will not be doing if it is quietly engaged with its chewtoys. It will not be chewing inappropriate household and garden items. It will not be a recreational barker. (It will still bark when strangers come to the house, but it will not spend all day barking for barking's sake.) And it will not be running around, fretting, and working itself up if left at home alone.

The wonderful thing about teaching a puppy to enjoy chewing chewtoys is that this activity excludes many alternative, extremely annoying puppy behaviors. A stuffed Kong is one of the best stress-relievers, especially for anxious, obsessive, and compulsive dogs. (A Kong for a dog is also one of the best stress-relievers for the owner.) There is no single device that so easily and so simply prevents or resolves so many bad habits and behavior problems.

Settle Down and Shush

A most pressing item on the educational agenda is to teach your pup that there are times for play and times for quiet moments. Specifically, to teach the youngster to settle down and shush for short periods. Your life will be more peaceful, and your pup's life will be less stressful once it learns that frequent little quiet moments are the name of the game in its new home.

Beware the trap of smothering your new puppy with non-stop attention and affection during its first days at home, for then it will whine, bark, and fret when left alone at night or during the daytime when you are at work and the children are at school. Of course the pup is lonely! This is its first time alone without its mother, littermates, or human companionship.

Chihuahua puppies are hardly Olympic destructive chewers, but they sure can yip. A stuffed Kong will teach it to settle down quickly, calmly...
...and quietly.

You can really help to ease your pup's anxiety by getting it used to settling down alone during its first few days at home. Remember, first impressions are very important and long lasting. Also keep in mind that the average suburban puppy will likely spend many hours and days left to its own devices. So it is well worthwhile to take the time to teach the pup how to spend time by itself. Otherwise, the puppy may become anxious when left alone and develop hard-to-break chewing, barking, digging, and escaping habits.

When you are at home confine your puppy to its doggy den with lots of chewtoys for housetraining, chewtoy-training, and teaching the pup to settle down peacefully and happily. It is important to confine your puppy for short periods when you are home in order to teach it how to enjoy its own company when left at home alone.

I am certainly not advocating leaving puppies alone for long periods of time. But it is a fact of modern day life that many puppy owners leave home each day to work for a living, so it is only fair to prepare the pup for this.

When you are at home, the key is short-term confinement. The idea is not to lock up the puppy for hours on end, but rather to teach it to settle down quickly in a variety of settings and be confined for variable, but by and large fairly short, periods.

To get your puppy used to settling down off-leash, tie a stuffed Kong to an eye-hook in the baseboard close to its bed next to the TV. It is easy to watch television and keep an eye on the pup at the same time. Do remember, though, the puppy still needs to be taken to its toilet area every hour.

Make sure that the only objects within reach are chewtoys stuffed with dry kibble and the occasional treat. Thus, the dog develops a strong chewtoy habit right from the outset, if only because there is precious little else at hand to chew. And let me repeat: A puppy happily preoccupied with a stuffed chewtoy is not destroying household articles and furniture and is not barking.

When you are at home it is also a good idea to occasionally confine your puppy to its puppy playroom (long-term confinement area) as a practice run for your absence. Occasional long-term confinement when you are at home allows you to monitor your pup's behavior so you have some idea how it will act when you are gone.

What to Do at Nighttime

You choose where your pup sleeps at night. If you want your pup in its long-term confinement area overnight, or in a dog crate in the kitchen, that's fine. Or if you want the pup (tethered) in its bed beside your bed, that's fine too. What is important, though, is that the puppy is confined to a small area and settles down quickly and quietly. Offer the puppy an intelligently stuffed chewtoy and it will likely chew itself to sleep in no time at all.

Once you have housetrained and chewtoy-trained your puppy and it has learned to settle down quickly and quietly, you may allow your pup to choose where it would like to sleep—indoors, outdoors, upstairs, downstairs, in your bedroom, or in your bed—just as long as its choice is fine with you.

It is a good idea to practice the nighttime routine during the daytime when you are awake and in a good humor, and not wait to train your puppy until you are tired and ready for bed and your grouchy brain is barely functioning. During the daytime,

Practice having your puppy settle down by your bed (or wherever you would like it to sleep at night) in the daytime, i.e., get your puppy used to sleeping peacefully alone before you plan to sleep peacefully.

practice having your puppy settle down in its bed or crate both in the same room as you and in different rooms so that it gets used to sleeping alone.

Should your pup whine at nighttime, check on it every ten minutes. Talk softly to it and stoke it gently for a minute and then go back to bed. However, do not overdo it. The idea is to reassure your puppy, not to train it to whine for late-night attention. Also, do not go straight to sleep, for you'll probably be checking on your puppy after ten minutes. Once the puppy eventually falls asleep, I find it enjoyable to check in on it and stroke it for four or five minutes. A lot of people dare not do this for fear they will wake the little critter, but it has always worked well for me.

If you follow the above routine, you'll find it will take less than seven nights before your puppy learns to go to sleep quickly and quietly.

Sit, etc.

I guess there would be more than a few disappointed owners if I didn't at least say something about training your dog to sit. Well, it's just so easy. Ask your puppy, "Would you like to learn to sit on request?" and then move a piece of kibble up and down in front of its nose. If your puppy nods in agreement, then you're both ready to proceed.

Say "Puppy, Sit," and then move the kibble upwards and backwards along the top of its muzzle. As the puppy looks up to follow the kibble, it will sit down. Pretty simple, yes?

Now say "Puppy, Down," and with another piece of kibble between finger and thumb, lower your hand (palm downwards) to just in front of the dog's two forepaws. Your pup will lower its nose to investigate the kibble and then lower its forequarters with the side of its muzzle on the floor to nuzzle under your hand. Move the kibble slightly towards your puppy's chest, and its rear end will plop down.

Now say "Puppy, Stand," and move the kibble forwards away from your puppy. (You may have to waggle the kibble a little to reactivate the pup.) Hold the treat at nose level, but lower it a tad as soon as your pup stands up and starts to sniff; otherwise your pup will sit as soon as it stands.

Say "Puppy, Sit," waggle a food lure in front of its nose and then raise the lure (palm upwards) just a little. As the puppy looks up to follow the lure it will sit down. Praise the pup, "Good Sit," and offer the food as a reward.

Say "Puppy, Down" and then lower the lure (palm downwards) to just in front of the pup's forepaws. The puppy will lower its nose to follow the lure and then lie down. Praise the pup, "Good Down," and maybe offer the food as a reward.

87

Now try chaining a few commands together. Back up a couple of steps, say "Puppy, Come Here," and wave the kibble. Enthusiastically praise your puppy as it approaches, and then ask it to sit and lie down before offering the kibble. Three responses for one piece of kibble—not bad, aye? Now have your puppy come, sit, and lie down as many times as there are spare moments in the day or as many pieces of kibble in the dog's dinner.

Say "Puppy, Stand," and then move the food lure away from the pup's nose and waggle it. Praise the pup as soon as it stands up, "Good Stand," and maybe offer the food as a reward.

Repetitively practice the above three position changes in random sequences, e.g., Sit, Down, Sit, Stand, Down, Stand. See how many position changes your pup is willing to do for just one food reward and how long you can keep the puppy in each position (short stays) before giving each food reward. Strangely enough, the fewer treats you give and the longer you keep each treat in your hand, the better your pup will learn. Welcome to the wonderful world of lure/reward training.

Misbehavior

Misbehavior is sadly a most prevalent terminal illness for pet dogs because many puppies all but sign their death warrants during their very first week at home. Minor housesoiling and chewing mistakes lead to banishment to the back yard, where the dog develops severe socialization problems and learns to bark, dig, and escape. By the time the dog is picked up on the streets as an escapee or a latch-key stray or is surrendered to an animal shelter, it has developed so many behavior problems that it is not easily adoptable.

Sadly, all of these utterly predictable problems could be so easily prevented by basic common sense, owner education, and puppy education.

Puppy Priorities

Once you have completed your doggy education and chosen the best possible puppy, you will find there is much to do and little time to do it. Here are your puppy priorities listed in order of urgency and ranked in terms of importance.

1. Household Etiquette
(From the very first day your puppy comes home)
Housetraining, chewtoy-training, and teaching your dog alternatives to recreational barking are by far the most pressing items on your puppy's educational agenda. From day one, employ errorless management teaching programs, comprising confinement schedules plus the liberal use of chewtoys (Kongs, Biscuit Balls, and sterilized longbones) stuffed with kibble. Simple behavior problems are so easily preventable, yet they are the most common reasons for people's dissatisfaction with their dogs and the most common reasons for dog euthanasia. Teaching household manners should be your number one priority the first day your puppy comes home.

#1 Urgency Rating
Household etiquette is by far the most pressing item on your new puppy's educational agenda. If you want to avoid annoying behavior problems, training must begin the very first day your puppy comes home.

#3 Importance Rating
Teaching household etiquette is extremely important. Puppies quickly become unwelcome when their owners allow them to develop housesoiling, chewing, barking, digging, and escaping problems.

2. Home Alone

(During the first few days and weeks your puppy is at home)
Sadly, the maddening pace of present-day domestic dogdom necessitates teaching your puppy how to enjoy spending time at home alone—not only to ensure your pup adheres to established household etiquette when unsupervised, but more importantly to prevent your puppy from becoming anxious in your absence. Normally, these go hand in hand; for when puppies become anxious they tend to bark, chew, dig, and urinate more frequently. From the outset, and especially during its first few days and weeks in your home, your puppy needs to be taught how to entertain itself quietly, calmly, and confidently. Otherwise it most certainly will become severely stressed when left at home alone.

#2 Urgency Rating
Teaching your pup to confidently enjoy its own company is the second most urgent item on its educational agenda. It would be unfair to smother the puppy with attention and affection during its first days or weeks at home, only to subject the pup to solitary confinement when the adults go back to work and children go back to school. During the first few days and weeks when you are around to monitor your puppy's behavior, teach it to enjoy quiet moments confined to its puppy playroom or doggy den. Especially be sure to provide some form of occupational therapy (stuffed chewtoys) for your puppy to busy itself and enjoyably pass the time while you are away.

#3 Importance Rating
Preparing your puppy for time alone is extremely important both for your peace of mind, i.e., preventing housesoiling, chewing, and barking problems, and especially for your puppy's peace of mind. It is absolutely no fun for a pup to be over-dependent, stressed, and anxious.

3. Socialization With People

(Always, but especially before twelve weeks of age)

Many puppy training techniques focus on teaching your puppy to enjoy the company and actions of people. Well-socialized dogs are confident and friendly, rather than fearful and aggressive. Show all family members, visitors, and strangers how to get your puppy to come, sit, lie down, roll over, and enjoy being handled for pieces of kibble. Living with an undersocialized dog can be frustrating, difficult, and potentially dangerous. For undersocialized dogs, life is unbearably stressful.

#3 Urgency Rating

Many people think that puppy classes are for socializing puppies with people. Not strictly true. Certainly puppy classes provide a convenient venue for socialized puppies to continue socializing with people. However, puppies must be well socialized towards people before they attend classes at twelve weeks of age. The time-window for socialization closes at three months of age, and so there is some urgency to adequately socialize your puppy to people. During your pup's first month at home, it needs to meet and interact positively with at least one hundred different people!

#2 Importance Rating

Socializing your puppy to enjoy people is vital—second only in importance to your pup learning to inhibit the force of its bite and develop a soft mouth. Socialization must never end. Remember, your adolescent dog will begin to desocialize unless it continues to meet unfamiliar people every day. Walk your dog or expand your own social life at home.

4. Dog-Dog Socialization

*(Between three months and eighteen weeks of age
to establish reliable bite inhibition and forever after
to maintain friendliness to other dogs)*
As soon as your puppy turns three months old, it is time to play catch up vis-a-vis dog-dog socialization, time for puppy classes, long walks, and visits to dog parks. Well-socialized dogs would rather play than bite or fight. And well-socialized dogs usually bite more gently, if ever they should bite or fight.

#4 Urgency Rating

If you would like to have an adult dog who enjoys the company of other dogs, puppy classes and walks are essential, especially since many puppies have been sequestered indoors until they have been immunized against parvovirus and other serious doggy diseases (by the very earliest at three months of age).

#6 Importance Rating

It is hard to rate the importance of dog-dog socialization. Depending on the lifestyle of the owners, dog-friendliness may be an unnecessary or an essential quality. If you would like to enjoy walks with your adult dog, early socialization in puppy classes and dog parks is essential. Surprisingly, though, very few people walk their dogs. Whereas large dogs and urban dogs tend to be walked quite frequently, small dogs and suburban dogs are seldom walked.

Regardless of the desired sociability of your adult dog, dog-dog play and especially play-fighting and play-biting during puppyhood are absolutely essential for the development of bite inhibition and a soft mouth. For this reason alone, puppy classes and trips to the dog park are the top priority at three months-of-age.

5. Sit and Settle Down Commands

(Begin anytime you would like your puppydog to listen to you)
If you teach your dog just a couple of commands, they would have to be Sit and Settle Down. Just think of all the mischievous things your puppydog cannot do when it is sitting.

#5 Urgency Rating

Unlike socialization and bite inhibition which must occur during puppyhood, you may teach your dog to sit and settle down at any age, so there is no great urgency. However, because it is so easy and so much fun to teach young puppies, why not start teaching basic manners the very first day you bring your puppy home, or as early as four or five weeks if you are raising the litter? The only urgency to teach these simple and effective control commands would be if ever your puppy's antics or activity level begin to irritate you. Sit or Settle Down will solve most problems.

#5 Importance Rating

It is difficult to rate the importance of basic manners. Personally I like dogs which can enjoy being dogs without being a bother to other people. On the other hand, many people happily live with dogs without any formal training whatsoever. If you consider your dog to be perfect for you, make your own choice. But if you or other people find your dog's behavior to be annoying, why not teach it how to behave? Indeed, a simple sit prevents the majority of annoying behavior problems, including jumping-up, dashing through doorways, running away, bothering people, chasing its tail, chasing the cat, etc., etc. The list is long! It is so much easier to teach your dog how to act from the outset, i.e., to teach the one right way (e.g., to sit), rather than trying to correct the many things it does wrong. Regardless, it would be unfair to get on your dog's case for bad manners if it is only breaking rules it didn't know existed.

6. Bite Inhibition
(By eighteen weeks of age)

A soft mouth is the single most important quality for any dog. Hopefully, your dog will never bite or fight, but if it does, well-established bite inhibition ensures that your dog causes little if any damage.

Socialization is an ongoing process of ever-widening experience and confidence building that helps your pup to comfortably handle the challenges and changes of everyday adult life. However, it is impossible to prepare your puppy for every possible eventuality, and on those rare occasions when adult dogs are badly hurt, frightened, scared, or upset, they seldom write letters of complaint. Instead, dogs customarily growl and bite, whereupon the level of bite inhibition training from puppyhood predetermines the seriousness of the damage.

Adult dogs with poor bite inhibition rarely mouth and seldom bite, but when they do, the bites almost always break the skin. Adult dogs with well-established bite inhibition often mouth during play, and should they bite, the bites almost never break the skin because during puppyhood the dog learned how to register a complaint without inflicting any damage.

Bite inhibition is one of the most misunderstood aspects of behavioral development in dogs (and other animals). Many owners make the catastrophic mistake of stopping their puppy from mouthing altogether. If a puppy is not allowed to play-bite, it cannot develop reliable bite inhibition. Pups are born virtual biting machines with needle sharp teeth so that they learn biting hurts before they develop the jaw strength to cause appreciable harm. However, they can not learn to inhibit the force of their bites if they are never allowed to play-bite and play-fight.

Bite inhibition training comprises first teaching the puppy to progressively inhibit the force of its bites until painful puppy play-biting is toned down and transformed into gentle puppy mouthing, and then, and only then, teaching it to progressively inhibit the incidence of its mouthing. Thus the puppy learns that mouthing is by and large inappropriate and that any pressured bite is absolutely unacceptable.

#6 Urgency Rating

You have until your puppy is four and a half months old, so take your time to ensure your puppy masters this most important item in its educational curriculum. The more times your puppy bites, the safer its jaws will be as an adult since it has had more opportunities to learn that biting hurts.

If you are worried about your puppy's biting behavior, enroll in a puppy class immediately. You may seek further advice from the trainer, and your puppy may let off steam and redirect many of its bites towards other puppies during play sessions.

#1 Importance Rating

Bite inhibition is of crucial importance, by far the single most important quality of any dog, or any animal. Living with a dog that does not have reliable bite inhibition is unpleasant and dangerous. Bite inhibition *must* be acquired during puppyhood. You must fully understand how to teach your puppy. Attempting to teach bite inhibition to an adolescent or adult dog is often extremely difficult, dangerous and time-consuming. Research the book and video lists at the end of this booklet and consult a trainer immediately.

To learn about your puppy's next three Developmental Deadlines, you need to read *AFTER You Get Your Puppy*. This booklet is available at no cost when you enroll in SIRIUS Puppy Training classes (1-800-419-8748) in the San Francisco Bay Area. Several other pet dog training schools include the booklet (or an order form) in Registration Packets for puppy classes. To locate a Certified Pet Dog Trainer (CPDT) in your area, please contact:

The Association of Pet Dog Trainers
1-800-PET-DOGS

AFTER You Get Your Puppy may be purchased directly from:
James & Kenneth Publishers
www.jamesandkenneth.com
1-800-784-5531

The Most Important Things to Teach Your Puppy

1. Bite Inhibition
2. Socialization with People
3. Household Etiquette
3. Home Alone
5. Sit and Settle Down Commands
6. Dog-Dog Socialization

The Most Urgent Things to Teach Your Puppy

1. Household Etiquette
2. Home Alone
3. Socialization with People
4. Dog-Dog Socialization
5. Sit and Settle Down Commands
6. Bite Inhibition

Books and Videos

Most bookshops and pet stores offer a bewildering choice of dog books and videos. Consequently, a number of dog training associations have voted on what they consider to be the most useful for prospective puppy owners. I have included the lists as voted by the Dog Friendly Dog Trainers Group. Also included in parentheses are the ranks as voted by the Association of Pet Dog Trainers (APDT)—the largest association of pet dog trainers worldwide, and by the Canadian Association of Professional Pet Dog Trainers (CAPPDT).

Most of the books and videos are practical puppy raising guides, primarily comprising useful training tips and techniques. In addition, I have included lists of my own: a list for those of you who especially want to have fun with your dog, and a list for those of you who are interested in a better understanding of dog behavior and psychology.

TOP FIVE BEST VIDEOS

#1 Sirius Puppy Training - Ian Dunbar
James & Kenneth Publishers, 1987. (CAPPDT #1, APDT #1)

#2 Training Dogs with Dunbar - Ian Dunbar
James & Kenneth Publishers, 1996. (CAPPDT #2, APDT #4)

#3 Training the Companion Dog (4 videos) - Ian Dunbar
James & Kenneth Publishers, 1992. (APDT #2, Winner of the Dog Writers Association of America *Maxwell Award* for Best Dog Training Video)

#4 Dog Training for Children - Ian Dunbar
James & Kenneth Publishers, 1996.

#5 Puppy Love: Raise Your Dog the Clicker Way - Karen Pryor & Carolyn Clark. Sunshine Books, 1999.

TOP TEN BEST BOOKS

#1 How to Teach a New Dog Old Tricks - Ian Dunbar
James & Kenneth Publishers, 1991. (APDT #1, CAPPDT #4)

#2 Doctor Dunbar's Good Little Dog Book - Ian Dunbar
James & Kenneth Publishers, 1992. (APDT #5, CAPPDT #6)

#3 The Power of Positive Dog Training - Pat Miller
Hungry Minds, 2001.

#4 The Perfect Puppy - Gwen Bailey
Hamlyn, 1995. (APDT #8)

#5 Dog Friendly Dog Training - Andrea Arden
IDG Books Worldwide, 2000.

#6 Positive Puppy Training Works - Joel Walton
David & James Publishers, 2002.

#7 Train Your Dog the Lazy Way - Andrea Arden
Alpha Books, 1999.

#8 Behavior Booklets (9 booklets) - Ian Dunbar
James & Kenneth Publishers, 1985. (APDT #9)

#9 25 Stupid Mistakes Dog Owners Make - Janine Adams
Lowell House, 2000.

#10 The Dog Whisperer - Paul Owens
Adams Media Corporation, 1999.

BOOKS/VIDEOS FOR DOGGY FUN

#1 Take a Bow Wow & Bow Wow Take 2 (2 videos)
Virginia Broitman & Sherri Lippman, Take a Bow Wow, 1995.
(APDT #5, CAPPDT #7)

#2 The Trick is in The Training - Stephanie Taunton & Cheryl
Smith. Barron's, 1998.

#3 Fun and Games with Your Dog - Gerd Ludwig
Barron's, 1996.

#4 Dog Tricks: Step by Step - Mary Zeigenfuse & Jan Walker
Howell Book House, 1997.

#5 Fun & Games with Dogs - Roy Hunter
Howlin Moon Press, 1993.

#6 Canine Adventures - Cynthia Miller
Animalia Publishing Company, 1999.

#7 Getting Started: Clicker Training for Dogs - Karen
Pryor. Sunshine Books, 2002

#8 Clicker Fun (3 videos) - Deborah Jones
Canine Training Systems, 1996.

#9 Agility Tricks - Donna Duford
Clean Run Productions, 1999.

#10 My Dog Can Do That !
ID Tag Company. 1991. The board game you play with your dog